WILLIAM · MATHIAS

Little Suite
for Piano

Music Department
OXFORD UNIVERSITY PRESS
Oxford and New York

Oxford University Press, Great Clarendon Street, Oxford OX2 6DP, England
Oxford University Press Inc., 198 Madison Avenue, New York, NY 10016, USA

Oxford is a trade mark of Oxford University Press

Duration: 6.5 minutes

Contents

1. Prelude

WILLIAM MATHIAS

Printed in Great Britain

OXFORD UNIVERSITY PRESS, MUSIC DEPARTMENT, GREAT CLARENDON STREET, OXFORD OX2 6DP

2. Dance

Allegretto (♩ = c. 144)

3. Celtic Lament

4. Burlesque

10

5. Arietta

Adagio semplice ($\quad$ = *c.* 66)

6. Finale